Beautiful America's
Oregon Coast

Beautiful America's
Oregon Coast

By Charlotte Dixon

Beautiful America Publishing Company

Front cover: A beautiful day at Cannon Beach from Ecola State Park

Opposite title page: Astoria Megler Bridge

Published by
Beautiful America Publishing Company
P.O. Box 244
Woodburn, OR 97071

Library of Congress Catalog Number 2007019679

ISBN 978-0-89802-838-6
ISBN 978-0-89802-839-3 (paperback)

Copyright 2007 by Beautiful America Publishing Company ©

All Rights Reserved
No portion of this book is to be reproduced
in any form, including electronic media
without written permission from the publisher.

Printed in Korea

Contents

Introduction 8

North Coast 13

Central Coast 31

South Coast 66

About the Author 78

Photo Credits 79

Sunset at Astoria Harbor

Lightship Columbia *at Columbia River Maritime Museum*

Astoria Column

Introduction

The Oregon Coast has a way of casting a spell over visitors. You'll come first, perhaps, for the spectacular scenery. The coast's majestic beauty is legendary and the terrain diverse, from vast sandy beaches, craggy capes crowned with towering ancient evergreens, rocky headlands, and even desert-like dunes. Once you've inhaled the sensory details of the landscape, you'll discover the amazing variety of things to do. Much of the coast has a charming rustic feel, with communities ranging from fishing villages and seasonal resorts, to artist's colonies. From Astoria at the northern end to Brookings down south, you'll experience historic lighthouses, soaring bridges, tasty seafood, amazing parks and natural areas, galleries, museums, and a world-class aquarium. And that's just for starters.

Beach activities alone could keep a person busy for an entire vacation. Seagulls call out news to each other and the distinctive fresh ocean smell fills the air. Long walks along the sand are always energizing, and you may want to treat yourself to beachcombing along the way. Shells and driftwood and other gifts wash up from the ocean regularly—and some coastal communities help the sea along by planting treasures of their own for visitors to find! Tide pools, with their fascinating variety of hermit crabs, starfish, and anemones are a family favorite.

Kite flying is popular along many stretches of sand all the way down the coast. If you prefer to look to the sea rather than the sky, whale watching might be your ticket. Experts are available at numerous locations along Highway 101 to answer your questions about the giant mammals and perhaps help you to see one. If you want to get even closer, you can charter a boat to whale watch on the water, or maybe you'd prefer deep-sea fishing. You can rent dune buggies or ride go-carts. There's hiking, bike riding, and world-class golf.

And that's just what's available at the beach itself. Oregon Coast towns offer a host of things to do and places to stay. Perhaps you'll fall in love with one community in particular or want to explore them all. From the quaint art enclave of Cannon Beach to the bustle of Lincoln City, down to the "banana belt" of Brookings-Harbor, the variety of coastal cities truly does offer something for everyone. Shop at stores ranging from fancy boutiques to outlet malls featuring fantastic deals. Visit art galleries or sip your morning latte in one of many friendly coffee shops. Eat pizza with the kids or enjoy a romantic evening out, indulging in a lavish gourmet dinner. Stay in a funky beachside cabin or a five-star hotel which offers all the amenities from massage to exercise rooms. Or perhaps you'll want to camp at one of Oregon's well-maintained state parks. Even there you have choices, from tent camping to RV parks, to renting a fully furnished yurt.

You may want to bask in the sunlight of a shimmering summer day, when you can while away golden hours frolicking on the beach or poking around town. Or perhaps you'll prefer to glory in the ferocious energy of a winter storm. There's nothing cozier than sitting before a blazing fire, with a cup of hot chocolate or tea, and watching the pounding surf and howling winds from your safe and dry vantage point.

Something that Oregonians are very proud of is the fact that all 363 miles of ocean beach are public and open to all. Over all those miles of sand and rocky headland you'll find no fences, no developments, not a single *No Trespassing* sign in sight. This is thanks to the foresight of an early Oregon governor, Oswald West. In 1913 he passed legislation making all of the state's beaches public. "No selfish local interest should be permitted, by politics or otherwise, to destroy or even impair this great birthright of our people." So said Governor West in 1913, and the beaches remain open to all. The legal tenet was reaffirmed with the passage of the Beach Bill in 1967, and a Supreme Court decision in 1969.

One note: many first-time visitors to the Oregon Coast are lured by its beauty but have no idea of the power of the ocean. Native Oregonians and long-time residents of the coastal areas have learned to respect the sea and live in harmony with it, and you can too, if you keep in mind a few simple

Shore birds at Cannon Beach

The annual Sand Castle Contest at Cannon Beach

Opposite page: The Needles at Cannon Beach

guidelines. Never turn your back to the ocean—sneaker waves are completely unpredictable and so are rip currents. Don't climb on logs you might see on the beach—the ocean can easily pick one up and deposit it on top of you. And be aware that high tides have been known to trap people on secluded beaches or headlands. Always know whether the tide is coming in or going out. Free tide tables are available all up and down the coast, at information centers and many restaurants. Odds are good that your place of lodging will have one for you to study (and they are worth perusing—there's something fascinating about the ebb and flow of the tides).

Our itinerary as we explore the myriad delights of the coast will take us along the twists and turns of Highway 101, which runs the length of the coast. 101 was designated Oregon's Pacific Coast Scenic Byway in 1998, and it was named an All American Road, one of only 21 in the nation, in 2001. We'll begin at the northern end of the state, by the Washington border, and end our tour at the California border to the south. Along the way we'll take you through all the stunning scenery and memorable experiences the Oregon Coast has to offer.

As you explore the coast, you'll notice unique and interesting names for locations. Many place names are based on the language of the region's original residents—the Native Americans, who first inhabited the area 12,000 years ago! They lived a peaceful, subsistence existence, building canoes to travel the coastline, estuaries and rivers to fish for salmon and hunt seal, duck, and game and gather fruits and berries. Along the North Coast, the Tillamook and Siletz tribes lived, while the Central Coast was home to the Siuslaw and Alsea. Coos and Coquille Indians flourished on the South Coast. Several museums along the way feature exhibits which further explain this fascinating bit of coastal history as well as the role of the Spanish and British explorers who followed.

After taking this tour, maybe you'll want to consider extending your visit to the beach permanently. Many cities along the coast are becoming retirement meccas, and city chambers and visitor's associations can assist you with relocation services. But whether you are scouting for a new home, or simply seeking a relaxing vacation, you'll find what you're looking for on the Oregon Coast.

Ready? Then grab your sunscreen and a fleece jacket, as the weather is changeable in every season. Bring sunglasses and a raincoat, and most important, a spirit of adventure. There's so much to do and see, so let's get going.

North Coast

We'll begin our Oregon Coast experience with a stop in the city of Astoria, the Grande Dame of the North Coast. A beautiful city full of charming Victorian homes, historic buildings, and friendly people, Astoria is located along the Columbia River a few miles from the Pacific. The city is picturesque, spreading up hilly terrain in a manner reminiscent of San Francisco, which has made it a favorite location for filmmakers. As the Clatsop County seat, it boasts a population of nearly 10,000 people, the largest city in the county, and it has become a destination for a wide variety of vacationers, including cruise ship passengers, river runners, and history buffs.

You'll catch gorgeous views of the Columbia River from many vantage points throughout Astoria, and you can also stroll the city's historic waterfront, where you can observe barges and freighters beginning their trek upriver, and watch commercial fishing boats unload their daily catch. If your feet get tired, hop on the riverfront trolley, "Old 300." A restored 1913 streetcar, the trolley carries visitors between the Port of Astoria and the East Mooring Basin, a four-mile ride. You'll enjoy listening to stories about Astoria, told by the all-volunteer crew of motormen and conductors. After your trolley ride, downtown stores and restaurants offer a variety of shopping and eating experiences, and while there, be sure to admire the recently restored Liberty Theater.

Not only enchanting visually, and full of things to do, the city is also historically significant. It is the oldest settlement west of the Rocky

The beautiful coastline south of Cannon Beach

Sea stacks near Garibaldi

Mountains, and was a rich fur-trading, salmon and timber center in the 1800s. Astoria has a unique claim to fame—it has more buildings on the National Historic Register per square foot than any other place in Oregon! Captain Robert Gray first landed here in 1792, Lewis and Clark arrived in 1805, and the city celebrates this history with many places to visit and learn more about it. The town itself is named for one of the earliest fur traders to locate here, John Jacob Astor.

Museums highlighting Astoria's history are many and diverse. The Columbia River Maritime Museum is the official maritime museum for the state of Oregon and it is chock full of exhibits about the area's rich seafaring legacy. The museum is a must-see for its extensive collection of nautical artifacts. The Firefighters Museum delights young and old alike with its collection of firefighting equipment and memorabilia and photos. And a stop at the Capt. George Flavel House Museum is a must. The home was built in 1885 and is considered a stellar example of Queen Anne architecture. The spacious interior features 14-foot ceilings, and six fireplaces. It is set on expansive grounds covering a city block, and serves as a glimpse into how the wealthy of the era lived.

No visit to the city is complete without a stop at the Astoria Column, which stands 125 mighty feet tall atop Coxcomb Hill, overlooking the city. As you might imagine, the view from the top is magnificent, encompassing the Pacific Ocean, mountain ranges in both Oregon and Washington, the Columbia River, and, of course, the city of Astoria. The column was built in 1926 to promote commerce and travel by the *Great Northern Railway*. Decorated with an Italian art form named sgraffito which combines carving and painting, the scenes on the concrete structure depict events from the tumultuous history of the Pacific Northwest.

Before we take our leave of this fascinating city, there's one more aspect of it to explore, and that is Astoria's rich association with Hollywood. The town's picturesque quality has made it a favorite location for many movies. One of the most loved films shot here was *The Goonies*, a childhood (and adult!) favorite for several decades now.

Cape Falcon from Oswald West State Park

Goonie enthusiasts can visit the house where the movie's heroes Mikey and Brand lived, as well as many other locations from the film. Another special film was *Free Willy*, which has a unique Oregon Coast connection. Keiko, the whale featured in the film, spent some of his life at the Newport Aquarium on the central Oregon Coast, before he was returned to Iceland and the freedom of the seas. Other films shot in and around Astoria include *Come See The Paradise*, *Kindergarten Cop*, and *Teenage Mutant Ninja Turtles III*. The Clatsop County Historical Society offers information about Astoria movie locations, including a tour book.

Now turning our attention in a southward direction, we'll cross Young's Bay and pass through Warrenton, a small town bursting with recreation areas and bustling marinas. Here you'll find Fort Stevens State Park, yet another site rich in historical significance. Once the site of a thriving Indian village, the United States army later built a fort and a series of bunkers at this location, to defend the mouth of the Columbia River. It has the distinction of being the only military installation in the continental United States to have been fired on since the War of 1812. On the night of June 21, 1942, a Japanese submarine fired 17 shells at the fort. Fortunately, nobody was injured and no damage was incurred.

Nowadays, Fort Stevens offers extensive hiking and biking trails and miles of sand dunes, as well as year-round camping facilities. Come summer, historical battles are reenacted. The park also includes 20th century gun batteries leftover from its military days and a history museum. On the beach you can view the wreck of the *Peter Iredale*.

A bit further south is Fort Clatsop, famous for its association with the Lewis and Clark Expedition. Fort Clatsop was the winter encampment of the Corps of Discovery from December 1805 to March 1806. The park includes an interpretive center and a fascinating replica of the Fort itself. Worth noting is the fact that the original fort had rotted away by the mid-1880s. Because the area receives an average of 70 inches of rainfall a year, untreated wood (as Lewis and Clark used) rots quickly! Much to everyone's shock and dismay, the original Fort Clatsop replica burned to the ground in October 2005. However, a new and better replica rose again in spring of 2006. It was built with the help of numerous volunteers and was based on new research into the fort's original appearance. After visiting the Fort exhibits, you may want to walk the Fort to Sea trail, a six-mile route to the ocean which Lewis and Clark established. In 2005, to celebrate the bicentennial of the expedition's journey, Fort Clatsop and Fort Stevens were combined to create a new national park: the Lewis and Clark National Historic Park.

Now that your mind is full up of historical facts and figures, perhaps you might like a break for some good old-fashioned fun. Driving further south on 101, we'll first pass the residential community of Gearhart, which is known for its grand old vacation homes. Across the Necanicum River Estuary we'll head into fun-loving Seaside, which has many festive delights to offer vacationers. The beach here stretches south from the Estuary all the way down to the craggy majesty of Tillamook Head. Sunbathing, kite-flying, and long strolls are all favorite activities. At low tide, try your skill at clam digging. All it takes is a bucket and a shovel! Best bets for success with clams are minus tides in spring and autumn.

If the sand is too difficult to walk in consider meandering instead along the Prom, a two-mile walkway built in the 1920s, which parallels the beach for the length of the city. Benches dot the walk, so you can take a load off and admire views of the ocean on one side, or grand old Seaside homes on the other. Where the Prom meets the city's main street of Broadway you'll find the Turnaround, a roundabout anchored by a statue of—who else?—Lewis and Clark. Head down Broadway to peruse a festive variety of candy shops, gift stores, arcades and restaurants. There's even a carousel for youngsters of all ages to ride.

The Seaside Museum offers historic photos and a unique viewpoint on this amusement-filled town. The Seaside Aquarium is worth a visit, too. A beloved local landmark built in the 1920's, it was first used as a saltwater swimming pool until its conversion to an aquarium in 1937.

And, now that you've had a bit of a break from history, we're going to

Cape Meares Lighthouse

Cape Meares State Park

pull you back into it with one more attraction. You can't leave Seaside without viewing the Lewis and Clark Salt Works. This marks the spot where the Corps of Discovery set up camp to boil sea water for their stay at Fort Clatsop as well as their return journey east. While salt may seem inconsequential to us, or something we try to use less of on our food, it was of great importance to Lewis and Clark, as they used salt to cure meat. The members of the expedition ate about 10 pounds of meat per day, so you can see why extracting salt to preserve it was a high priority.

It's now time to pull yourself away from the delights of Seaside and head south on Highway 101 once again. Take a slight side trip inland when you reach the junction of 101 and Highway 26 (the road in from Portland). Just three miles east you'll see signs for the Largest Sitka Spruce Tree, which lives in Klootchy Creek Park. It's well worth a stop to see this giant spruce. Foresters have determined that the tree is 750 years old. It is 216 feet tall and has a circumference of over 56 feet, which are simply numbers on a page until you get up close and witness the grandeur of this tree. A viewing platform is built around its base, making it easy to admire the tree's huge trunk. This spruce was designated Oregon's first Heritage Tree, which recognizes trees for their connection to Oregon history. The Sitka Spruce was an unknown species until Lewis and Clark discovered and noted it on their expedition.

We have many more wonderful places to visit along the North Coast. Our next stop will be Cannon Beach, nestled between the Coast Mountain Range and the Pacific Ocean. Famous for its miles of beautiful, sandy beaches marked by forested headlands, the town is an art-lover's heaven as well. Cannon Beach got its name from a cannon that washed ashore from the shipwrecked *USS Shark* in 1846. At the northern end of town, follow signs to Ecola State Park. Drive up a winding road through Oregon rain forest until you reach a parking lot and picnic area with stunning ocean views. Well-maintained trails lead to Indian Beach, and the area is a bird-watching mecca, with interpretive signs explaining what species you'll be likely to see here.

This is also a great whale watching spot. To the untrained eye, the waters of the Pacific seem placid, but beneath the surface they are churning with life, and you'll find that Oregon Coast residents are avid whale watchers. If you've never spotted a whale breaching the water before, or witnessed some of their acrobatic shenanigans, you're in for a treat. During three official whale watching weeks each year in December, March, and August, Ecola and more than 30 other sites down the coast are staffed with volunteers who can help you spot whales and give you all kinds of information about them. Simply look for the "Whale Watching Spoken Here," signs. Here's an advance preview of some facts about the gray whale. Every year 18,000 gray whales swim a 10,000-mile migration between Alaska's Bering and Chukchi seas to lagoons in Baja California, where they mate and give birth before heading north again. Long ago, whalers named the gray whale "Devil Fish" because of the ferocity with which they guarded their young, but these days the whales are known for their friendliness to people. These gentle mammals are gigantic—adults average 45 feet in length and weigh 70,000 pounds!

After your visit to Ecola, you'll probably be eager to get your toes into the sand of those beaches you saw from on high. Drive on into town and you'll find numerous public beach accesses. It's worth noting that the beach here was recently chosen as one of the "world's best" by the Travel Channel. The town's famous landmark, or perhaps it should more rightfully be called a seamark, is Haystack Rock, at 235 feet the world's third largest monolith. (Its accompanying, smaller monoliths are cleverly named The Needles.) The fact that Haystack was granted Marine Garden status by the US Department of Fish and Wildlife in 1990, means marine and animal life is strictly protected. The rock is a favored nesting ground for ocean birds, and the rocky tide pools at its base are especially fun to explore at low tide. Look for colorful starfish, anemones, crabs, chitons and sea slugs.

Gaze out to sea a little to the north and you'll see the Tillamook Rock Lighthouse. Oregon has a number of restored lighthouses, many of them open to visitors with interpretive displays and interesting exhibits. Some

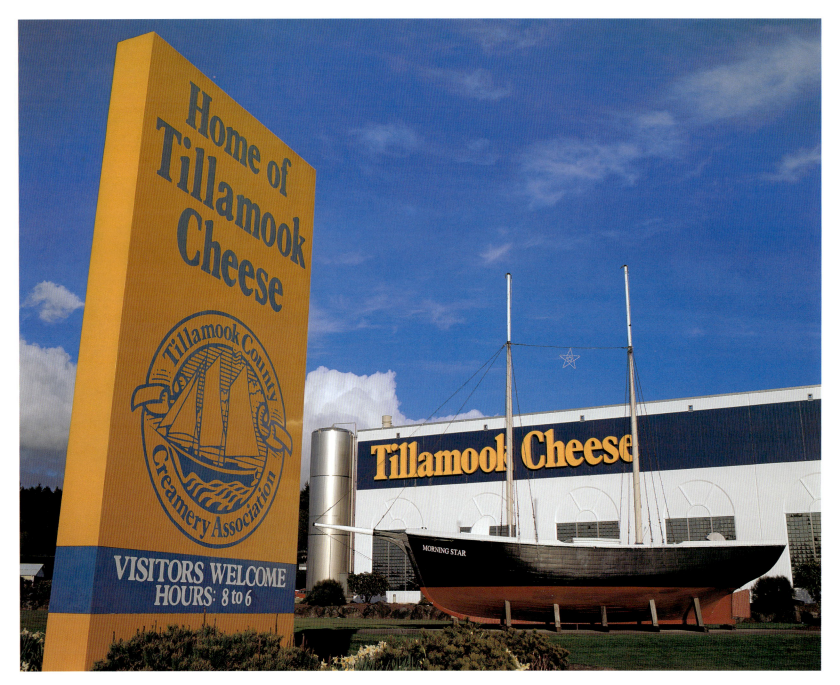

The home of Tillamook Cheese

Opposite page: Beautiful Cape Kiwanda with a rolling surf

also feature guided tours. Lighthouses have been called "Oregon's Sentinels," and they are highly visible links to the state's maritime heritage. Built on headlands or near major estuaries, most were established between 1870 and 1896 under the jurisdiction of the United States Coast Guard, which installed automatic beacons during the 1960s. This prompted restoration efforts to preserve these historic jewels and you'll see the fruits of those labors all along the coast. The Tillamook Rock Lighthouse is located on a rock a mile seaward from Tillamook Head. It was nicknamed "Terrible Tilly" because of its intense exposure to ocean waves. This is the only privately owned Oregon Coast lighthouse on the National Register of Historic Places, and is now the *Eternity at Sea* columbarium, a place to lay to rest ashes of the deceased.

As you walk the beaches in the area of Cannon Beach, you'll notice all manner of festive, colorful kites flying above you. It's such a popular activity here that it has its own kite festival every April. Another well-known and well-loved activity is the annual Sandcastle Day, held each June. You'll be amazed at the variety of creatures and structures and original ideas that arise out of the sand! Only natural materials are allowed, which adds to the fun and creativity.

Once you've gotten your fill of the beach, never fear, there is much to do in town. Known as a haven for art and artists, many art galleries dot the main street of Hemlock, interspersed with boutiques and cafes selling pizza, ice cream, salt water taffy, and baked goods (c'mon, you can indulge a little after all that walking on the beach!). When it's time to rest for the evening, you'll find a variety of lodging ranging from luxury inns to inexpensive motels.

Resuming our tour south, we'll wind our way past Oswald West State Park (named for the beloved governor who first insured that the beaches would remain public) and Neahkahnie Mountain. Hikers will want to trek to the top of the mountain, but the less dedicated walkers can still enjoy spectacular views from the many roadside turnouts as the highway skirts the mountain. These viewpoints are also great whale watching spots. Next you'll drive through Manzanita, Nehalem and Wheeler, three charming towns strung like jewels along Highway 101. Each offers its own delights, from the lovely white-sand beach, quaint vacation homes and golf course at Manzanita, the charm of Nehalem's location on the Nehalem River, to the historic feel of Wheeler, where you can enjoy a Crab Festival come June. Nehalem Bay State Park offers a variety of activities, including a 6-mile horse trail and a boat ramp, which offers access to fishing and crabbing. We're into Tillamook County now, famous for its dairy cows and the products those cows produce—cheese and ice cream.

Next up is Rockaway, a town of 1,200 built in the 1920s by Portland residents who desired a summer resort. Here, seven miles of sandy beaches await you, as well as shops and restaurants and many fun activities. And a stop in Garibaldi is a must on everyone's list. The small port town is located on Tillamook Bay, and is a gateway for fishing charters, crabbing, clamming and other water sports. It's a pleasure to wander amongst the boats and if you happen to visit the town in May, you will witness the Blessing of the Fleets. Don't miss the unique Garibaldi Museum, which is dedicated to telling the story of Captain Robert Gray, who in 1792 discovered the Columbia River and named it after his ship.

And now our route on 101 takes us into Tillamook. But before we head into the town proper, we'll stop first at the Tillamook Cheese Visitor's Center. Here you can enjoy a free self-guided tour, taste cheese samples (num!) and browse in the gift and gourmet shops. Observation areas allow first-hand viewing of the cheese-making process. Tillamook cheese is produced by an almost century-old farmer's cooperative, whose founders laid down core values that are still followed today. Many people would say you can taste the cooperative's devotion to integrity in their delicious cheeses and creamy ice cream.

Crossing the Wilson River, bridge aficionados will want to pause and admire the bridge. It is one of a series of bridges all along the coast designed by Conde McCullough. As the state bridge engineer from 1919 until his death in 1946, McCullough constructed over 600 bridges

Cape Kiwanda State Park

The view south from Cascade Head

throughout Oregon, filling in many gaps in the state's road and highway system. McCullough's goal was to elevate bridge design and make crossing a bridge something special and he succeeded, as his bridges are known throughout the world. His coastal bridges are considered his crowning achievements and he himself called them "jeweled clasps in a wonderful string of matched pearls." The Wilson River Bridge is the first of several we'll cross on our coastal tour, and it is noteworthy for its bowstring arch design.

The city of Tillamook is a thriving center for the county's agricultural activities. It is the county seat (and it must be noted here that Tillamook County boasts more cows than people) and the supply center for the dairy industry. Just south of town, you'll find the Tillamook Air Museum, which is home to a massive World War II blimp hangar which houses a collection of rare World War II aircraft that still fly!

Now we're going to detour off our chosen north-south route of Highway 101 in order to take in the stunning scenery and the lovely beachside communities along the Three Capes Scenic Loop. The capes in question are Cape Meares, Cape Lookout, and Cape Kiwanda. Head west from the center of Tillamook and this scenic road will take you past all three capes. It's a side trip that won't disappoint.

Cape Meares is the northernmost point of this route, and the day-use state park there boasts exceptional views. Worth stopping for is the Cape Lookout Lighthouse, the shortest one on the coast. It was first illuminated in 1890 and replaced by automatic beacon in 1963. Trails lead from the parking area to the lighthouse and viewpoints overlooking rocky islets, where, with luck, you'll catch glimpses of sea lions sunning on the rocks and nesting seabirds.

Also nearby is the Octopus Tree, an unusual Sitka spruce featured in Ripley's Believe it or Not. Cape Lookout State Park is spread over 2000 acres, and offers 200 campsites, as well as yurts and cabins. You might see hang gliders and paragliders practicing their sport here. At Cape Kiwanda, the awesome forces of nature are highly evident as the wind and water have created a unique headland. Please note that this Cape is best appreciated from the beach. Beautiful as it is, it is dangerous to explore on foot.

Several beach communities might strike your fancy as you drive this loop. Oceanside is a small town near the Arch Rocks National Wildlife Refuge. Pacific City is known for the dory boats that are launched directly into the surf. Pass this way in July and you'll have the pleasure of experiencing Dory Days. After connecting back to Highway 101, you'll notice the community of Neskowin. Though mostly residential, the town's art scene packs a wallop, with an art gallery, the Neskowin Chamber Music series, and the nearby Sitka Center for the Arts and Ecology at Cascade Head.

Cascade Head, too, is the unofficial border between the North Coast and the Central Coast. Just as many varied and unique delights await us as we continue our adventure on the Central Coast.

Central Coast

Ah, Lincoln City, the crown jewel of the Central Coast. Not only is it a favorite resort destination for generations of Oregonians, it is also a bustling city. Located on the 45th parallel, Lincoln City has so many activities, both on the beach and in town; you'll want to stay as long as possible to enjoy them all. The current incarnation of Lincoln City was born in 1965, when the five communities of Oceanlake, Delake, Taft, Cutler City and Nelscott banded together. The city's name was chosen from a suggestion made by local school children in a contest to determine a new name for the combined towns.

There are seven miles of beachfront here, and the skies above many of them will no doubt be festooned with brightly colored kites. The winds are highly favorable for kite flying, so much so that *KiteLines Magazine* named Lincoln City the Kite Capital of the World. This distinction is celebrated with Kite Festivals in May and September and you'll find many shops catering to this sport in town. Believe it or not, the city has also sponsored

Kite flying at Lincoln City

an Indoor Kite Flying Festival.

Another unique activity along Lincoln City beaches is searching for glass floats. Yes, glass floats. Beachcombers of a certain age will remember when these green and blue beauties would wash ashore from Japanese fishing vessels, where they were used to anchor nets. Finding one was considered the ultimate prize of a beachcomber's quest. These days, however, most fishing floats are made of plastic, and so the precious glass floats have become a thing of the past—except on the beaches of Lincoln City. Every October, and continuing into May, more than 2000 beautiful glass floats are set out, a few placed each day that weather permits. The number of floats coincides with the year. So, 2000 were put out in 2000, 2001 in 2001, and so on. The hand-made floats are set out all along the seven miles of beaches, above the tide lines and below the beach embankment. If you are one of the lucky ones to find a float, you may call the Visitor's Center to register it. In return, they'll send you a Certificate of Authenticity, along with information about the artist who created it.

But never fear, if you are disappointed in your search for a glass float, you may learn how to make one yourself at the Jennifer L. Sears Glass Art Studio. They offer classes in creating your own glass float or paperweight, as well as daily glass-blowing demonstrations. Two other glass studios in town, Glass Confusion and Alder House III combine to make the city a mecca for those who want to learn this ancient and mysterious craft.

Lincoln City offers an array of charming small shops and boutiques. The neighborhoods of Oceanlake, Delake, Taft, and Nelscott all have enclaves of specialty shops ranging from antiques to delectable chocolates and candies. And for shopping on a grander scale, try the Tanger Outlet Center, home to more than 65 well-known stores.

For another kind of indoor sport, many visitors love the casino. The Chinook Winds Casino Resort at the north end of town features a full-service hotel, two restaurants, top-name entertainment, a video arcade for the youngsters, and, yes, all the casino games adults love.

If the sun is shining (or even if it's raining—the natives never let a little

Beautiful Driftwood Creek Covered Bridge

Boiler Bay State Park

rain stop them), your pockets are full of cash from your winnings, and you're craving a different sort of outdoor experience, head to Devil's Lake, just a short distance from the city's core. Canoe or kayak while you see all kinds of birds—coots, cormorants, ducks, loons, bald eagles and grebes are just some of the species you might find. The park gives kayak tours during the summer. There's a campground on the west side of the lake, and a day use area on the east side. While there, be sure to check out the world's shortest river, the D River. Its length of 120 feet connects Devil's Lake with the Pacific Ocean.

Regretfully, it's time to leave the outdoor and indoor fun of Lincoln City behind. However, many other wonderful places await us as we continue our journey south. Next up is Depoe Bay, an utterly picturesque town perched above the ocean. The town likes to call itself a "fairy tale fishing village," and it's easy to see why, as the entire city core is bursting with charming shops and boutiques. Because a huge sea wall runs the entire length of the downtown area, visitors shop or dine with the ocean always in sight.

You'll be able to view one of Depoe Bay's claims to fame, its spouting horns, from anywhere along the seawall. On windy days at high tide, waves run beneath shoreline lava beds, spurting seawater 60 feet into the air. Watch this spectacular sight from one of the cafes or fine restaurants in town, many of them serving fresh seafood, perhaps caught by one of the many deep-sea fishing boats that depart from Depoe Bay. The town lays claim to having the world's smallest navigable harbor, and fishing charters depart from it every day at dawn, laden with passengers eager to catch cod, rockfish, Chinook and Coho salmon and the delicious Dungeness crab.

If fishing isn't your thing, how about a whale-watching tour? Those, too, depart from the harbor. You can hop aboard a comfortable cruiser or a zippy Zodiac for an up-close encounter with the giant mammals. You're almost guaranteed a sighting, as Depoe Bay has a resident pod of gray whales, which makes its home there ten months out of the year. Never fear—if the thought of boarding a boat makes you seasick, but you've got a yen to see whales, you'll have a good chance of sighting them from the Seawall, which is staffed by volunteers during Whale Watching Weeks.

This town is no stranger to special events, either. Town folk are nearly always preparing for one festivity or another. There's the Memorial Day Fleet of Flowers, the Indian Style Salmon Bake in September, and the Magic of Christmas in December, when the town tree is lit amid caroling and beautiful seasonal decorations.

Even the town's name has an interesting origin. The land the town now sits on was allocated by the United States government in 1894 to a Siletz Indian man named Charlie Depot. He in turn had gotten his name from his employment at an army depot. The family later changed the spelling of the name to Depoe, and that spelling was adopted when the first post office was established on the site in 1928.

A short way south of Depoe Bay is the Devil's Punchbowl State Natural Area, and is worth a visit. This is a location of fascinating geography. The punchbowl is a hollow rock formation which was created by the collapse of a roof over two sea caves. Wave action has further shaped it, and during winter storms, ocean water froths and roars and mixes into a thrilling violent brew in the punchbowl. There is a picnic area here, and it is a popular spot for whale watching.

And now, on to Newport, which has been a favorite vacation spot since 1856, and it's easy to see why. Cozily situated between the Coast Mountains, the Pacific Ocean and Yaquina Bay, it is a picturesque city loaded with things to do and sights to see. The town's early beginnings are responsible for creating two very distinct areas. There's the Historic Bayfront near the center of town, and Nye Beach.

At the start of the 20th century, Nye Beach was the most popular attraction on the whole coast. The Sea Bath Sanatorium drew many visitors. This facility was built by Dr. Henry Minthorn (President Herbert Hoover's uncle). Bathers thought that the hot baths de-toxified poisons from the body. Today Nye Beach continues to be a hip destination, with the Newport Performing Arts and Visual Arts Center proudly nestled

"The World's Smallest Harbor" – Depoe Bay

A charter fishing boat enters Depoe Bay

The stormy coastline near Depoe Bay

among bookstores, art galleries, restaurants and lodging. It's a casual, friendly area, with a village-like atmosphere and lots of nooks and crannies to explore.

Especially noteworthy is the Sylvia Beach Hotel, "a hotel for book lovers." Rooms are divided into three categories: classics, best sellers and novels, and each one is decorated in homage to a well-known author. You could stay in the Willa Cather room, or how about the Edgar Allen Poe or Alice Walker? Meals are taken family style, with everyone eating together. Watch out—one of the dining room's favorite activities is a little after-dinner game of Two Truths and a Lie. Play it once and you'll be hooked—both on the game and the camaraderie of the hotel.

Newport's Bayfront area is a short distance away, and in summer a shuttle operates between the two areas, passing popular attractions along the way. Historically, the Bayfront once housed a port for timber and fishing activities. Today it is still a working waterfront, home to one of Oregon's largest fishing fleets. It's also a delightful place for visitors to stroll, replete with shops, restaurants, and fish-processing plants in turn-of-the-century storefronts. There's fun for the whole family at attractions such as Ripley's Believe It or Not, the Wax Works museum, and the Undersea Gardens.

No visit to Newport is complete without taking in the attractions devoted in one way or another to marine life. There's the Hatfield Marine Science Visitor Center at the South Beach Marina, a research facility for the study of the ocean and estuary. It offers interesting exhibits about marine animals and even includes a touch tank. And then there's the Oregon Coast Aquarium, which is rated as one of the top ten aquariums in the country. Enjoy watching otters, seals, and sea lions swim in viewing pools and walk a path to the sea aviary and tufted puffin display. You can also walk beneath the sea in a submerged 200-foot acrylic tunnel, where you'll thrill to be face to face with sharks and other mysterious sea creatures.

Newport is the proud home of not one, but two lighthouses. The Yaquina Head Lighthouse is three miles north of town and it stands 162 feet above sea level. The Yaquina Bay Lighthouse is a museum you'll enjoy visiting, and a great whale-watching spot. It is the second-oldest standing lighthouse structure on the Oregon Coast. It features a museum open daily except for major holidays. The Yaquina Bay Bridge is another beauty built by Conde McCullough. It crosses the bay and features five concrete support decks leading to a dramatic steel arch. There are pedestrian plazas with observation areas at each end of the bridge and from the north end, a steep street will lead you back down to the Bayfront.

The Newport area is home to many special events, as you might imagine. Chief among them is the Newport Seafood and Wine Festival, held every year along Yaquina Bay across from the Bayfront. This festive event attracts more than 17,000 visitors every year. They come for the chance to sample wine from Washington, Oregon and California, beer, gourmet food from the region's top chefs, and stroll among the arts and crafts booths. All told, more than 120 exhibitors participate.

We're going to take a short detour off Highway 101 to visit the small town of Toledo, seven miles up a scenic drive paralleling the Yaquina River, with river and estuary views, wonderful bird watching, and bike and hiking paths. Upon arrival at Toledo, you'll find the drive has been worthwhile. Toledo was once a busy mill community, but now it is a town full of antique, yarn, and craft shops. Many are located along the town's charming Main Street, which still retains an historic feel. From the center of town, you can see fishing boats moored on the waterfront a short distance away. Many well-known artists make their home here, no doubt compelled by the wooded hills surrounding the town, and the bucolic river and rural vistas. When it's windy at the beach, Toledo is often warm and sunny, so it's definitely worth a visit.

Back on Highway 101 after this brief detour, we'll once again head south. Passing through the residential community of Seal Rock, you'll notice chainsaw sculptures by a local artist. And then the road goes over the Alsea Bay Bridge, newly completed in 1991. With a clearance of 70 feet, the piles that support the bridge reach more than 100 feet into the bedrock

Fishing fleet at Newport Harbor

Opposite page: Otter Rock from Devil's Punchbowl State Park

below! At the south end of the bridge is the Historic Alsea Bay Bridge Interpretive Center, worth a stop to learn more about area transportation, coastal bridges and the bay.

Waldport is a community of over 2,000 nestled on the bay. It's a haven for fishing, crabbing, and clamming and even features a free crabbing dock. A little further south, you'll find the town of Yachats, which likes to call itself "the gem of the Oregon Coast." And no, the name does not rhyme with hatchets. The correct pronunciation is YAH-hots, from the Chinook Indian word Yahuts, which means "dark waters at the foot of the mountain." It's a small village of only 635 people, but it's a beauty—nestled between the Coast Range and the Pacific, its location affording many scenic views. At the northern end of town you'll find Smelt Sands State Park, where the smelt run down the Yachats River every year. (It's not a well-known fact, but the Yachats River Estuary is a great place to catch cutthroat trout.) Visit Yachats in July and you'll be treated to an all-you-can-eat Smelt Fry, complete with rolls, coleslaw, pickles, chips, fries, sausage, and pie. While enjoying the unique taste of smelt, you'll be entertained by old-time fiddlers and a German Umpa band.

Three miles south of "downtown" Yachats is the Cape Perpetua Scenic Area. This 2,700-acre area is part of the Siuslaw National Forest, and more than 20 miles of trails loop through it. At 802 feet, the Cape Perpetua Overlook is the highest viewpoint on the coast so close to the ocean—hence a place of thrilling views. On a hike you'll be awed by majestic old-growth trees and dizzying views of the crashing surf below. Pause for a moment to witness the Devil's Churn. A fissure in the basalt bedrock allows ocean water to crash through it in a spectacular sight.

Next stop is Heceta Head Lighthouse, perched on the west side of Heceta Head 205 feet above the ocean. The lighthouse, with its 56-foot tower, was first illuminated in 1894 and the automated beacon can be seen 21 miles from land. This earns it a rating as the strongest light on the Oregon Coast. The lighthouse is open for tours daily from May to September and the historic assistant light keeper's house offers bed and breakfast and group rentals. The Cape Creek Bridge is a McCullough design with two-tiered viaducts modeled on Roman aqueducts. Nearby Devil's Elbow beach has restrooms and picnic facilities, and is the best place to take in the full beauty of the bridge. Trails offer a variety of hiking options—from a leisurely one-mile round trip stroll to a very strenuous eight-mile hike.

We're heading down the road to Florence, but first up is another one-of-a-kind attraction—the Sea Lion Caves. This natural cave is the world's largest sea cave and home to a huge number of Steller Sea Lions. It's hard to wrap your mind around, but the formation of the cave began about 25 million years ago! The cave now reaches the height of a 12-story building and spans the length of a football field. In the fall and winter, sea lions gather in the natural amphitheater. A visit in spring and summer will still bring you ample sighting opportunities, as the sea lions breed and tend their young on rock ledges just outside the cave.

The Steller Sea Lion is a warm-blooded mammal, sometimes also called an eared seal. Worldwide, there is a population of 80,000 sea lions, of which a herd of 200 typically makes its home at these caves. Interestingly, the only known natural enemy of the sea lion is the killer whale, but most of the time sea lions can scramble out of the water onto a rocky haven and reach safety. Unfortunately, man has also been a threat to the safety of sea lions, but at the Sea Lion Caves great care has always been taken to preserve the mammal's natural habitat. Access to the caves is by elevator, which was built in 1961. However, it is worth noting that, to reach the elevator, visitors must walk down (and back up) 37 steps, as well as 400 yards of uphill and downhill trails. Seeing the sea lions is well worth it, though. The caves are open every day of the year except for Thanksgiving and Christmas Day.

Further south on our route, plant lovers will relish a stop at the Darlingtonia State Natural Site. This 18-acre park was created to preserve and showcase the rare carnivorous Darlingtonia plant also known as the Cobra Lily or Pitcher Plant, which is indigenous to southern Oregon and

"Old Man and the Sea" mural, Newport

Yaquina Bay Lighthouse (1871) Newport

northern California coastal areas. You'll enjoy a walk on the loop trail which overlooks verdant patches of Darlingtonia. With luck you'll see this plant in action, luring an insect with its smell, then trapping and digesting it.

And now we reach Florence, the last stop on our tour of the Central Coast of Oregon. This town of almost 8,000 was recently named the number one retirement community in the country by Retirement Places Rated. It's easy to see why. While the city features all the modern amenities anyone could ask for, it also has historic charm, and it's surrounded by incredible beauty and fun recreational opportunities, including two 18-hole golf courses. You definitely won't want to miss the Old Town district. Located on the Siuslaw River, this is a vibrant district replete with shops, restaurants and activities, many of them located in historic buildings.

As this district attests, Florence has much historic significance. Originally inhabited by the Siuslaw Indians, the first Europeans came when Spanish galleons charted the territory. Years later the English sailor Captain Cook sailed the coastline, naming many areas as he went. Florence derives its name from a French ship that went aground near the mouth of the Siuslaw River. The first white people arrived for good in 1826 when Hudson Bay Traders established an outpost, and in 1876 the first cannery was established.

The Siuslaw Pioneer Museum is an informative stop for those who wish to learn more about coastal history. It features an Indian dugout canoe, blacksmith's bellows, and even a steam engine! Docents are on hand to answer questions and talk about the artifacts on display. The avid fisherman will not want to miss the Fly Fishing Museum in Old Town. On display are thousands of flies collected from over 20 countries. Some date back to the 1800s.

After poking around the shops and museums, save some time, because there is much more to see. You'll cross the Siuslaw River Bridge, which was built in 1936 by Conde McCullough to replace ferry service across the river. Bridge enthusiasts will delight in the art deco details on the four guardhouses. Best views are from downtown Florence. Just south of town

Beautiful Yaquina Head Lighthouse

Underwater passage at the Top 10 Oregon Coast Aquarium

Children love the Puffins at Oregon Coast Aquarium

Everyone enjoys the friendly Otter pups at Oregon Coast Aquarium

Seal Rock State Park

The outstanding view south from Cape Perpetua

Classic Heceta Head Lighthouse, north of Florence

Sunset at Devil's Elbow, Heceta Head Lighthouse State Park

Fabulous Sea Lion Caves, north of Florence

Opposite page: Sand dunes at Heceta Beach looking south

Oregon Dunes National Recreation Area

Umpqua Lighthouse, Winchester Bay

Fishing boats at Charleston Harbor

Beautiful dahlias at Shore Acres State Park

Shore Acres, beautiful from every direction

Opposite page: Shore Acres State Park with Cape Arago Lighthouse in the distance

Sunset and sea stacks at Bandon

Beautiful Bandon Beach

Coquille River Lighthouse, Bandon

Cranberry harvest time at Bandon

Cape Blanco Lighthouse (1870) oldest standing on the coast

begin the dunes—40 miles of them, many over 300 feet high, and the largest span of coastal dunes in the United States. They were created from millions of years of wind, sun, and rain erosion. The Oregon Dunes National Recreation Area stretches from Florence to Coos Bay. Private companies such as Sand Dune Frontiers offer tours on Giant Dune Buggies or thrilling rides on their Sand Rails. A favorite among locals and visitors alike is Jessie M. Honeyman Memorial State Park, which is the second largest overnight camping park in the state. There are two miles of dunes between the park and the ocean for you to explore. And there are three lakes: Woahink, which has a boat dock, swimming and picnic facilities, Cleawox, with wheelchair accessible trails, and Lily.

And with this, we'll say goodbye to our Central Coast idyll. Never fear, though, because the South Coast has much to recommend it also, including beautiful stretches of coastline and banana-belt weather. Let's head further south!

South Coast

Reedsport and its neighbor, Winchester Bay, are known as the "Heart of the Oregon Dunes." In Reedsport you'll find the Oregon Dunes National Recreation Area headquarters, with information on the area's natural history, recreation opportunities, and many exhibits. Also well worth a visit is the Umpqua Discovery Center, where you'll enjoy extensive dioramas depicting the history of the various groups of people who have settled in the area and how the Umpqua River affected them. There's also a working weather station, an operational periscope, and a scale model of a sawmill. The Umpqua River is the second largest in the state. The Umpqua River Bridge is one of the more unique McCullough bridges, as it is the largest span bridge in Oregon. Span bridges themselves are somewhat unusual, as they move side to side instead of up and down. A little east of town, the Dean Creek Elk Viewing Area is worth the short three-mile drive. It features lush pastures and woodlands full of wildlife.

Winchester Bay, located where the Umpqua River meets the Pacific Ocean, features Salmon Harbor, with room for 900 fishing boats and many fishing charters available. Shops, lodging, cafes and art galleries surround the harbor. Nearby you'll find the Umpqua River Lighthouse. The first lighthouse located here fell into the river in 1861 when sand eroded beneath the structure! This current lighthouse is still operational and is accessible only through tours given May through October. Right across the road is the Umpqua River Whale Watching Station, a stellar spot for, you guessed it, whale watching.

Our next stop is actually three stops in one. The cities of Coos Bay, North Bend and Charleston are collectively known as the Bay Area, and you'll find much to delight and entertain you in each. North Bend is the northern gateway to the Bay Area, and fittingly, the city has a magnificent symbol of this, the mile-long McCullough-designed Bridge which spans the bay. When built, it was the longest bridge in Oregon, and this green steel beauty is actually named the Conde B. McCullough Memorial Bridge in honor of the prolific engineer. The downtown area has many shops and galleries to visit, and the town is also the home of the Pony Village Mall, the largest indoor shopping center on the coast. For those casino lovers, there's The Mill Casino. North Bend was originally named Yarrow, after either the plant, a river in Scotland, or a vessel, nobody is entirely sure which. Its current name is more fitting, as the city is located on the north bend of the Coos Bay channel. North Bend was historically the base of operations for timber baron Asa M. Simpson and his son Louis. Today it is home to nearly 10,000 people and a Coast Guard air station.

Coos Bay is the largest of the three Bay Area cities; it is the commercial center of the South Coast, and the largest city on the coast. The downtown area has recently been renovated and is nearby the Coos Bay Boardwalk. Charleston, on the ocean entrance to Coos Bay, is the area's fishing center, with sport and commercial fishing featured. The Oregon Institute of Marine Science is located here, as well as a Coast Guard Lifeboat Station.

Beach at Port Orford looking south to Humbug Mountain

Sea stacks at Arch Point, south of Pistol River

As you continue along your tour, you'll want to stop at Shore Acres State Park. The location of the estate of timber baron and developer Louis Simpson, his original mansion is gone, but spectacular botanical gardens remain. Simpson brought flowering plants from all over the world to cultivate at his five-acre garden. Spread atop a cliff overlooking the ocean, during the winter holidays the grounds light up with more than a quarter-million lights. As you might guess, Shore Acres is also a fabulous place to view whales.

In Bandon, you'll find a charming and picturesque community, the entirety of which was rebuilt in 1936 after a devastating fire destroyed the business district and most of the residencies. The one remnant of the former city is a brick chimney from an old bakery which serves as a memorial. It is located just off Highway 101. Today, the Old Town district along the Coquille River waterfront pulses with galleries, shops, and cafes. It's adjacent to the town boat basin from which there are excellent ocean views. At Bullard Beach State Park, you can see the Coquille River Lighthouse, which was built in 1896, decommissioned in 1939, and is the process of being restored today. This lighthouse has the distinction of being one of the few ever hit by a ship, which happened in 1903, when an abandoned schooner collided with it during a storm.

You'll want to drive the Beach Loop Road, which passes by many interesting rock formations or sea stacks, including the Garden of the Gods, Elephant Rock, and Table Rock. The most famous, however, is Face Rock, which legend says is the face of an Indian maiden frozen to stone by evil spirits. Nearby Cat and Kittens Rock were her pets, cast into the sea by the same nasty spirits.

Bandon is the Cranberry Capital of Oregon, and the bogs are visible as you drive south of town. The crop averages about 30 million pounds of berries annually, which equals five percent of the nation's cranberries and 95% of the Oregon harvest. The cranberry industry got its start here in 1885, when a transplant from Massachusetts, Charles McFarlin, planted vines he brought from his home. This original bog produced cranberries for eighty years, with the variety obviously adapting well to conditions along the Oregon Coast. Today, the principal variety grown in the area is named after McFarlin.

Golfers may be familiar with Bandon for its golf course. Bandon Dunes is a world-class golf course with sweeping views of the untamed coast—similar to the very place the sport was born, in Scotland. It is quickly establishing itself as a top destination for golf.

South of Bandon lies Port Orford. At over a century and a half old, the town is the oldest on the Oregon Coast, and it had its start when Captain William Tichenor established a settlement to supply miners. In the 1920s, the cedar industry took off in the area. It also has the distinction of being the most westerly city in the continental United States. Today the town is a fishing village and artist and retirement community. Who wouldn't want to settle here? There are gorgeous beaches and hiking trails, an artsy air with many galleries owned by working artists, and numerous gift shops. At the Port Orford Lifeboat Station Museum, there is shipwreck memorabilia and even a restored Coast Guard station. The port of Port Orford is also worth a visit. It is the only natural, open water port for 600 miles and only one of six "dolly" ports in the world. You'll be awed to watch working fishing boats lifted into and out of the water. Late afternoon is a good time to visit the dock, as this is when fishing boats return to shore to unload their catch.

From Port Orford to Brookings on Highway 101 is a stunning stretch of endless magnificent vistas. You'll be within view of the ocean for most of the 60-mile drive. However, don't pass up the town of Gold Beach without stopping. Named for the gold that was found here in the 1800's, Gold Beach is 50 miles north of the California border, situated where the Rogue River meets the sea. It is the heart of "America's Wild River Coast." There's world-class fishing here all year, including salmon, steelhead, trout, and ocean charters available for lingcod, rockfish and the delicious Dungeness crab. Here, too, you'll see the last of the McCullough bridges. This one crosses the Rogue River and was the first in the country to be built

Spring at Samuel H. Boardman State Park from Indian Sands viewpoint

Natural Bridge Cove, Boardman State Park

using a special method of employing pre-stressed concrete.

There's mild weather here, and many recreational opportunities. A chief draw is riding Jet Boats up the Rogue River. Departing from the Gold Beach dock is the only way to reach the Wild and Scenic portion of the Rogue, and it's a wild and wonderful ride! The jet boats are specially designed to navigate through rapids and strong currents. Trained river pilots will regale you with tales of the river, and you'll see incredible scenery and wildlife, including black bear, otters, eagles, and mountain lions. Most excursions include lunch or dinner stopovers at upriver lodges. There's also an option for an overnight stay at the lodges, which offer elegance amidst a peaceful setting.

Our tour of the Oregon Coast ends at its southern border, at the town of Brookings-Harbor. Situated at the conflux of the Chetco River and the Pacific Ocean, this city is known as the "banana belt" of the Oregon Coast, as it has the warmest average temperatures. It may well surprise you to learn that daytime temperatures can reach 70 to 80 degrees here during any month of the year. For this and other reasons, it is a fast-growing community, with many retirees and a booming real estate market. Because the region is home to many commercial flower growers, a special treat in the spring and summer is to see their fields blazing with color. More than 90 percent of the Easter lilies grown in the United States come from this region, and in Azalea Park you'll see more than 1,000 varieties of flowering azaleas and rhododendrons. The Azalea Festival is held annually on Memorial Day weekend, and boasts a street fair and parade.

Though often referred to these days as Brookings-Harbor, the two are discreet towns. Harbor is an unincorporated community across the Chetco River from Brookings. At the Chetco Valley Historical Museum, visit the state's largest Monterey cypress tree, a 99-foot beauty, which was planted in the 1850s. Harris Beach State Park is an official Whale Watching Station. Other things to do in the area include fishing, camping, beachcombing and hiking.

And thus ends our amazing Oregon Coast tour. You've seen it all, from tall firs and majestic headlands, to endless sandy beaches and dizzying views of the Pacific Ocean. You've experienced the charm and friendliness and variety of coastal communities, and soaked up some history and local lore. Like so many others before you, you'll want to return to visit again and again, choosing a favorite destination or enjoying all the variety the coast has to offer. But watch out—if you're not careful the beautiful Oregon Coast may some day lure you back for good! The beauty and majesty of the Coast has that effect on people, which is why many one-time visitors now call the region home. Should that time come, the Oregon Coast will be waiting for you with open arms. In the meantime, it is yours to return to, revel in, and relax whenever you need a break from the hectic pace of contemporary life.

Wildflowers at Cape Ferrelo, near Brookings

Opposite page: Beautiful Harris State Park

About the Author
Charlotte Dixon

We couldn't have picked a better person to do the text for this book than our author, Charlotte Dixon. A free-lance journalist living in Portland, Oregon, her great-great grandparents were among the hardy pioneers who followed the Oregon Trail to settle in the West. She has had an affinity for the area all of her life.

With her heritage and extensive traveling in the state she has been able to impart that very important "first hand" knowledge that make her writings so enjoyable.

She has a degree in journalism from the University of Oregon and she is a past president of the Willamette Writers Association. She is kept busy contributing essays and profiles to a variety of local magazines and newspapers, while she continues to work actively to promote the literary arts in the Northwest.

Her association with Beautiful America Publishing Company has been steady. She wrote the text for, *Beautiful America's MAINE* and *Beautiful America's WYOMING*.

When she isn't busy at her hobbies of gardening, knitting, reading and hiking, she enjoys traveling with her family throughout the West and especially Oregon.

Photo Credits

DICK DIETRICH – *page 11 left; page 60; page 63; page 77*

CINDY HANSON – *page 50; page 51 left; page 51 right*

BRAD LA CHAPPELLE – *rear cover*

DIANNE DIETRICH LEIS – *front cover; page 2; page 6; page 10; page 14; page 39 right; page 43; page 46; page 49; page 54; page 55; page 58; page 59 left; page 61 left; page 61 right; page 62; page 64 left; page 72; page 73; page 80*

COURTESY OF LINCOLN CITY VISITOR & CONVENTION CENTER – *page 32*

PETER MARBACH – *page 7 right; page 15; page 24; page 28; page 56; page 64 right*

GEORGE VETTER/CANNON-BEACH.NET – *page 11 right.*

JAMIE & JUDY WILD – *page 7 left; page 20; page 25; page 34; page 38; page 39 left; page 47; page 52; page 59 right; page 65*

GEORGE WUERTHNER – *page 17; page 21; page 29; page 35; page 42; page 53; page 57; page 68; page 69; page 76*

A glorious pink and gold sunset at Brookings

Rear Cover: A huge wave crashes over the Tillamook Rock Lighthouse, now the **Eternity at Sea** *columbarium.*